MW01659757

SHIFT: LEADING IN TRANSITION

WORKBOOK

J.D. KING

Christos

Shift: Leading in Transition Workbook

Christos Publishing
Post Office Box 1333
Lees Summit, MO 64063

First Printing, in the United States, April 2021.
For Worldwide Distribution

ISBN: 978-1-950053-25-4

For other exciting releases from Christos Publishing visit our store:
www.TheResurgenceStore.com

"If you would not be forgotten, as soon as you are dead and rotten, either write things worth reading, or do things worth the writing."

—Benjamin Franklin

CONTENTS

PREFACE

"Anyone can hold the helm when the sea is calm." —Publilius Syrus

This workbook is designed for groups and individuals to reflect on principles documented in the book *Shift: Leading in Transition* by J.D. King. This study guide was not intended to be used alone; it functions best as a supplement. Use it along with the book.

This workbook does not merely mirror the text of Shift; it incorporates supplementary stories, questions, checklists, and practical engagement exercises.

Many workbooks include no additional data or stories. The reader is generally receiving the original text in a slightly different form with a few questions and lines to fill in. This workbook is not like that. It includes a number of added components.

I recommend you read the book and then turn to this workbook and reflect on what you have read. Many will read the chapter and then engage the corresponding portion of this study guide. That technique works well. But one can also read the entire book and then turn to the workbook. Either way works.

It is time for each of us to find ways to advance. Let's work together to find a way forward in the midst of a societal shift.

INTRODUCTION

I was talking with Richard about *Shift: Leading in Transition* and he asked if this book and workbook would help him. I told this business colleague that it probably wouldn't.

Richard was shocked. "J.D., didn't you tell me that I could get fresh insights and strategies from this? I'm confused."

I explained that he'd certainly benefit from *Shift* and its supplemental material, but only if he read it. I knew Richard long enough to be aware of his short attention span. He was too distracted to engage it.

I clarified that while this material could be beneficial. It probably wouldn't because of a surface level approach. One only gets out of something in proportion to what they are willing to put in.

He sighed and reluctantly agreed.

Books and study guides can help with personal growth and development, but they will only go as far as one lets them. Resources like this are merely tools. Without proper engagement, they will always fall short of the goal. The attitude and approach of the recipient determines the impact and reach.

Shift: Leading in Transition explores worldview, influence, and strategies for personal development. This supplemental workbook was designed to expand these efforts further. It includes applications, checklists, discussion points, and questions. Take your time and process all of this.

Before going over some particular action points from Shift, it is helpful to reflect on your mindset and expectations. Consider some of what you are bringing into this study.

- What prompted you to read *Shift: Leading in Transition*?

- What are you hoping to gain from engaging this book?

- What are some of the choices and life decisions that have led you to where you are now? Take a moment to reflect on a few of the major turning points in your life.

- For decades, innovation has opened the door to new ways of engagement and communication. What are some particular ways digital innovation has impacted our world?

- Many feel like the world is drastically changing in the post-COVID-19 era. What are some of the disruptions and reconfigurations that you've witnessed?

- Crises speed up changes already underway. What other disruptions do you anticipate seeing in the days ahead? How will these changes affect society?

- Has there been anything you have personally lost during this time?

- I told the story about my grandfather, Seldon Day (1895-1967), getting sick with the Spanish Flu in 1918. Do the pivotal stories of your family intersect with your life story?

Action Point

There are always "backstories" and "origin accounts" that you've never heard before. Take some time this weekend to call a parent or close relative. If possible, go and visit them in person.

Ask them to share their pivotal moments. Budget an hour or more to learn something that you've never heard before.

We're living during an era of transition and change. The world is not as it was a decade ago. It's important to keep asking questions and see where we stand in all of this.

- What kinds of issues should we consider as we move forward in this era?

Listening to stories and asking pivotal questions are exercises that leaders should never abandon. It is important for self-discovery and growth.

1

LEADING WITH A WEAK HAND

Sometimes we can lose our way and need help figuring things out. Fortunately, mature leaders can help us regain our stride and move forward. Some of the best leaders have told me meaningful stories.

Over the years, I had several conversations with Jim, an older Christian businessman. He recounted Bible stories and challenged my line of thought. Through him, I learned that the right kinds of stories enable us see things in a new light.

Whether you recognize it or not, our society is framed up by stories.

- Fairy tales comfort kids as they drift off to sleep.
- Allegiances with local sports teams extend the mythos of regional honor and shame.
- Family histories and ancestry DNA testing reveals hidden ethnic identities.
- Millions of interconnected fans "geek out" to television shows and blockbuster movies.
- Tiktok, Instagram, and social media channels enable

users to harness music, video, and imagery to curate and dramatize their lives.
- Narratives about injustice on television and social media incite outrage and political action.

People define their lives by the stories they tell and the narratives that they chose to believe. Not all of the stories that individuals embrace are true. It's important to consider what's transpiring around you.

Your Stories

> "Stories make, prop up, and bring down systems. Stories shape how we understand the world, our place in it, and our ability to change it. Humans have always used stories to make sense out of our chaotic world."—Ella Saltmarshe

You've been shaped by a number of different stories throughout your life. Your identity has been defined by family stories, biblical narratives, family histories, and Hollywood movies.

- Take a moment to briefly name some of stories that have influenced your life?

- What kind of patterns and common themes are found in these stories?

- I didn't learn enough about my grandparents and other godly leaders that I knew. Are there overlooked stories you should try to explore? Ask questions and see if you can find out what's missing.

- It's important to embrace the right kind of stories. These narratives become the lens by which we see the world around us. What do you believe about others and yourself? To borrow from the language of a Hollywood superhero movie, what is your origin story?

- When all is said and done, what do you want people to say about your life? What kind of story do you want told at your funeral?

My entrepreneur friend drew upon the story of King Asa from the Bible (2 Chronicles 15-16). Reflecting on the weaknesses of this leader, Jim highlighted three things: 1) Failure to remove the destructive things. 2) An improper relationship. 3) Refusal to trust in the power of God.

I found that it's helpful to go a little deeper into each of these points. The tension points in Asa's story have a lot to say to each of us.

Remove Things

"We spend a lot of time teaching our leaders what to do. We don't spend enough time teaching them what to stop."—Peter Drucker

In the Bible, God commissioned Asa to take down the wicked things in his nation. He made progress, even removing evil idols from his household. Yet, he couldn't complete the task.

It is hard to remove what we've grown accustomed to. People don't like to let go of the familiar. Sometimes, as a leader, you are bought into ideas, practices, and patterns. We fall in love with the tools and methods. This is normal.

But occasionally, the established order now inhibits the mission and must be revoked. Leadership is as much about subtraction as addition. Organizations need to stop doing what is unnecessary and destructive. Many times, leaders will need to remove more than they add.

Most of my ministry and business colleagues are always discussing the items on their "to-do list." I have one in hand and I'll bet that you do too. Everyone has tasks and projects that need attention, and most people write them down.

- What's on your mind right now? Get it off your mind and on paper in an actionable way.

To-do lists can be a vital leadership tool and should be regularly revisited. It is important to not only do the work, but also think about the work. Processing what's going on is part of the work.

However, leadership is not just about what needs to be done. It is also about what should be stopped. You probably have a to-do list, but do you have a stop-doing list? When you contemplate your areas of responsibility, invariably some things need to be discarded.

Example of a Stop Doing List:

- Stop underestimating personal connections.
- Stop discounting yourself or your team.
- Stop mediocrity.
- Stop criticizing and complaining.
- Stop listening to the haters and agitators.
- Stop confusing the urgent with the important.
- Stop ignoring valuable insights or concerns.
- Stop believing the worst about people.
- Stop losing focus.
- Stop being unclear about expectations.
- Stop living in the past.
- Stop living in the future.
- Stop taking people for granted
- Stop playing politics with people or the organization.
- Stop adding unnecessary complexity.
- Stop imposing unnecessary rules.
- Stope confusing the methods with the meaning.
- Stop wasting time and money on a dead end project.
- Stop assuming that you can see everything.
- Stop preferring a simple falsehood over a complex truth.
- Stop embracing style over substance.
- Stop allowing political ideologies to divide.
- Stop being prejudicial and ungracious.
- Stop being attracted to stories that justify wrong trajectories.

There are plenty of projects, ideas, and behaviors that would be in your best interest to stop.

- Take a moment to write a few of the things that you need to stop doing. Be ruthless.

- Think about your next course of action on these items. Write down your strategy.

Many times, clearing off the slate opens the door to personal growth and development. Leaders should be ready to remove everything that keeps people from finding their destiny.

An Improper Relationship

"Bad company ruins good morals" (1 Corinthians 15:33).

In telling this Bible story, Jim also highlighted an

inappropriate covenantal relationship. For short-term gains, King Asa formed a partnership with Aram, a wicked nation.

Since wrong relationships undermine everything, leaders have to be careful about who they partner with. They would never be closely associated with wrong individuals or institutions. Improper alignment destroys everything.

Intimate associations matter. We generally become like whoever we're aligned with.

Betrayed Mentor

James, a Midwestern law professor took a liking to one of his students. As he entered into private practice, he decided to take Mike under his wing. The experienced teacher unexpectedly gave his student full partnership in the firm.

James loved the idea of taking on a fathering role. He found it exhilarating to have someone in his life to champion. This role provided meaning and purpose. But James' compassionate heart blinded him to Mike's misguided ambitions. Believing in this young man, he ignored a multitude of red flags.

Although Mike always put on a good show, he didn't share the integrity or values of his mentor. Whenever the opportunity arose, he cheated and blurred the lines. In time, Mike exploited the circumstances and seized control of the firm. The student ultimately betrayed his teacher and forced him out of his own enterprise.

- Do you know anyone who suffered through a bad relationship?

- Have you established wrong relationships? How did these associations hinder you?

- If you sense that you treated others wrong and caused heartache, what are you going to do to clean up your messes? It's time to make things right.

- What can you do to establish healthier relationships moving forward?

Leaders that want to make a difference are intentional about their relationships. They learn lessons from their mistakes and find ways to make things better as they move forward.

Refusal to Trust in the Power of God

> "You know neither the Scriptures nor the power of God" (Matthew 22: 29).

One of the last things that Jim drew out of Asa's story was how he stood before God. When in trouble, the king should have sought help from the Lord. Even though he was sick, God was capable of aiding him. Asa just needed to petition his Heavenly Father. But the monarch did not move in that direction.

When leaders don't trust God to help, they don't experience all of the favor that has been afforded to them. Incredible things can happen, but they flow out of relationship and engagement.

- Why do you think people run away from God? What is going through their mind?

- Is seeking God's favor something you do regularly? Why or why not?

- Name a story, person, or experience that has influenced the way you look at God. How has this impacted you?

- If the people who knew you best heard you pray, what would be their impression of your faith?

- What are some particular ways that you can become closer to God?

Don't Let Your Hands Be Weak

Summing up his point, Jim told me, "Asa's story teaches us that a good man with weak hands can cause things to collapse. We must be strong where it matters."

Good intentions, or even a sincere desire for God, is not always enough. Leadership is not just about the matters of the heart. It also requires appropriate actions.

Anticipating some of his later problems, Asa was warned, "Be strong and don't let your hand be weak" (2 Chronicles 15:7). Apparently, he didn't listen.

- Are there any areas where your hands have been weak? Take a moment and reflect on this question.

- Provide a recent example of how your weakness has affected someone else. Nobody likes to write about these things, but it is important make honest assessments.

- How are you going to ensure that your hands are not weak in the days ahead? What are you going to do to position yourself for growth?

One of the ways to continue growing is to wrestle with stories, particularly the unpleasant ones. There is a lot to learn from the stories of misguided people in the marketplace, governance, and the church. We are going to briefly draw on this.

Weakness in the Marketplace

In the business realm, just like any other, leadership is crucial. Individuals making a difference in their field possess foresight and strength. They are transformational leaders.

Enterprise is expanding globally, but not all of it is rooted in competent leadership models. Many businesses will not survive in the coming years because the men and women guiding them are shortsighted.

Sears

Richard Warren Sears, a railroad operator, obtained reasonably priced goods in the 1890s and began marketing them. At this time, households traveled considerable distances for supplies. With limited supply chains, Sears captured people's intrigue with his merchandise.

Sears produced flyers to advertise his goods, and these promotional efforts expanded until he was mailed five-hundred-page catalogues. Sears' business exploded in rural communities with limited marketplace access. Families could now obtain goods though the post office and rail services, bypassing overpriced general stores.

In the second decade of the twentieth century, Henry Ford's Model T automobile disrupted the marketplace. With easier modes of travel, chain stores became more desirable to customers. So, the Sears and Roebuck Company continued to innovate, adding brick and mortar stores to their thriving catalogue business.

By 1969, Sears was the largest and most beloved retailer in

the world. They constructed a 108-story, 1,450-foot skyscraper in downtown Chicago. The Sears Tower—the tallest building in the Western Hemisphere—represented the company's innovation and adaption.

Sears was still prosperous in the closing decades of the twentieth century, investing in digital technologies and modernizations. But the board of directors rarely took seriously what the research and development teams were suggesting.

Even as the internet expanded in use during the late 1990s, Sears adapted surprisingly little. The old cutting-edge attitude of Richard Warren Sears was gone from the company. The leadership thought that their lifeblood came from their brick-and-mortar stores. Meanwhile, the company's biggest rival, Walmart, poured cash into emerging digital platforms. The trajectories of the two businesses couldn't be any more stark.

Although Sears had made billions, the company collapsed into financial free fall. By 2016, the ubiquitous company had lost $10.4 billion and was forced to file for Chapter 11 bankruptcy. One of the innovative and beloved enterprises in American history was no more. The Sears Tower is now named the Willis Tower in downtown Chicago.

- What information, critical to your organization, are you not paying enough attention to?

- What successful things are you doing today that may be blinding you to new growth opportunities?

- What emerging trends could make your current business model obsolete?

- How often does my organization assess its strengths, weaknesses, opportunities, and threats in order to understand the current social or business climate?

- Is your organization relevant? Will it be relevant five

years from now? Ten? Are you changing as fast as the world around us?

- Is my organization's long-term view reflected in its priorities? Do you effectively balance short and long-term priorities?

- How you would you reposition your organization if money was no object?

- What breakthrough could totally transform your field?

What is the most innovative thing that you can think of that would upend your industry?

Weaknesses in Politics

Elected officeholders are supposed to protect freedoms and extend the constructive elements of society. Through their efforts, safety and prosperity should grow. But that is rarely what comes to pass. Smiling politicians promise everything but deliver very little. Voters are hoping for visionaries but end up with bureaucrats with cheap theatrics and empty rhetoric.

Some of the stories of politicians demonstrate troubling patterns.

One example goes back to the American Civil War. Although a capable strategist, building an army of 70,000, General George McClellan was reluctant to attack. His lack of follow-through almost cost the Union the war.

- Are you holding back on any action points or blaming someone else for your unwillingness to advance? What's keeping you from moving forward?

Lies irreparably tarnish the prestige of a leader. Authorities should be held to a higher standard. There can be no deception amid twenty-first century leaders. This is an hour when honor must be restored.

- Do you struggle with telling the truth? Do you deceive those that you have been called to lead?

Are you so caught up in the details that you miss the big picture? Effective leaders don't let the methods distract them from the meaning.

- Like President Jimmy Carter, do you let the forms stand in the way of outcomes? Are you more caught up in the "how" than the "what"?

Even in difficult times, leaders should lead with clarity and definable benchmarks. Authorities during the COVID-19 pandemic have been inconsistent and unclear. Many don't know what they should do.

- Are you leading with clarity and sensible actions points? Does your team know how to advance?

Weakness in the Church

A hostile political environment, health scares, and social duress are contributing to the marginalization of congregations. There's no doubt about it. But what's truly obstructing the gospel's advance is ineffective leadership. Myriads of ministry heads have lost sight of their originating mission.

Without structural changes and a fresh stirring from God, the Christian witness will be significantly diminished in the West.

- Houses of worship are being disrupted by immense

social and political changes. How are the racial and demographic changes affecting organizations in the United States?

- How do you respond to political and social uncertainty?

- Are you stuck in a protectionist mindset, trying to hold on to what you have or are you looking to the future?

Over time, churches and nonprofits experience change.

Originating purposes are often forgotten as organizations age. Some people call this mission creep.

- Are you still aligned with your original mission or have things began to shift?

- While good intentions matter, so do appropriate actions. Are you doing what's necessary to move things forward in your organization? What actions are you prepared to make?

- Have you let arrogance and hubris affect you? Make an honest assessment.

What gets a leader to one level often will not take them to the next. Every new stage of development requires new modes of engagement. Organizations fail when leaders aren't willing to grow and adapt.

- Are you willing to pivot and do things differently?

First, we engage the stories, and then the stories have a way of engaging us. The unfolding narratives force us to see issues we'd prefer to overlook and disrupt our skewed trajectories. The narratives provide new vantage points and opportunities for readjustment. The old stories often provide the groundwork for brave, new exploits.

2

BEING AND DOING

Leadership is in the ongoing tension between *being* and *doing*. These dynamics are at play in anyone trying to establish a work. Leadership is built on a tension that never entirely lets up. Individuals carry some of this *push* and *pull* into a lifetime of service.

Leadership is made up of two central components—identity and action. Authorities influence people in their *being* and *doing*.

Being

> "People buy into the leader before they buy into the vision." —John C. Maxwell

Leadership is inexplicably rooted in one's *being*. Doing great things is part of the leadership quotient, but we must also understand the importance of *identity*. Leadership begins with who you are and what God is doing in you.

Authorities are called to speak and act, but words and actions are rooted in identity. Behavior exposes deeply entrenched *attitudes, experiences,* and *expectations*. A leader cannot escape the imprint of their essence.

Identity and Sonship

> "Know, first, who you are, and then adorn yourself accordingly." —Epictetus

Many leaders don't resolve the troubling emotional issues of their childhood. They don't realize that the past is still coloring their future.

- Are there issues from your past that affect how you lead and relate to people?

- Are there any negative emotions that drive your relationships or decision-making?

- What quirks are easy to spot in others, but difficult to spot in your life?

- What bad habits do you have? What justifications have you used to continue those habits? In what areas of your life do you need to be truthful right now?

- Do you have a healthy sense of identity? If not, why?

- What are the gaps in your knowledge and experience? How do you plan to rectify this?

Calling

> "The two most important days in your life are the day you are born and the day you find out why." —Mark Twain

Calling is a particular sense of mission that comes from God. Individuals should pursue whatever God has called them to accomplish. Calling is not about external markers but is rooted in larger life purposes.

The Olympic runner, Eric Liddell, was stirred by what surged inside him. As he ran, his soul teemed with life. A sense of calling and purpose should also arouse our hearts. What do you do that causes you to feel God's pleasure?

- What is your calling or vocation? What were you made to do?

- How are you developing and growing in your calling? What particular ways are you investing in your future?

Giftings

> "What I want to talk about now is the various ways God's Spirit gets worked into our lives. This is complex and often misunderstood, but I want you to be informed and knowledgeable." (1 Corinthians 12:1-2 MSG)

Over the years, people have recognized the remarkable favor of a few historical figures. Winston Churchill, Elvis Presley, and Ronald Reagan were all said to have charisma.

This term, in popular American vehicular, connotes a person with a likable demeanor, compelling tongue, and passionate temperament. But in the Bible, the term means an "infusion of grace." This idea is sometimes tied to "spiritual gifts."

Leadership is a gift that comes from God. It is a capacity that aligns with higher purposes. Even unbelievers unknowingly possess gifts from the throne room of heaven.

Individuals have different kinds of strengths and abilities. We could explore a number of personality and functional temperaments that people possess. That is not the goal of this exploration.

I prefer to look to the Bible. It points out various gifts and abilities from God. Take a moment and look through the following list:

- Word of Wisdom (I Corinthians 12:8; Luke 6:9).
- Word of Knowledge (I Corinthians 12:8; Luke 18:22).
- Faith: (I Corinthians 12:9; Acts 3:6-7).
- Gifts of healing (I Corinthians 12:9, 28; Acts 28:1-10).
- Working of miracles (I Corinthians 12:10; Acts 6:8).
- Prophecy (I Corinthians 12:10; I Thessalonians 5:20-21; Ephesians 4:11).
- Discerning of spirits (I Corinthians 12:10; Luke 8:29).
- Tongues (I Corinthians 12:10; Acts 19:6).
- Interpretation of tongues (I Corinthians 12:10; 14:13-33).
- Helping (I Corinthians 12:28).
- Administration (I Corinthians 12:28; Acts 6:2-3).
- Grace (Romans 12:6; Ephesians 3:7; 4:7; I Peter 4:10-11).
- Service (Romans 12:7; II Timothy 1:16-18).
- Teaching (Romans 12:7; Ephesians 4:11-14).
- Encouragement (Romans 12:8; Hebrews 10:24-25).
- Generosity (Romans 12:8; I Corinthians 13:3; Acts 4:32-35).

- Mercy (Romans 12:8; Luke 5:12-13).

Obviously, another item that should be included in this list is leadership. (see Romans 12:8; Acts 13:12.) Like many of the other abilities, the Bible considers leadership a spiritual enabling.

- What are some particular gifts and abilities that you have operated in?

- What do you imagine the gift of leadership looks like? Describe some of the qualities. Keep in mind that people lead in all different areas.

- How might leadership rooted in the grace and favor of God look different than other approaches?

We must remember that leadership is an outworking of grace and favor, not a product of education, manipulation, or self-promotion. Effective rule comes from a place outside of us.

Development

> "There is nothing noble in being superior to your fellow man; true nobility is being superior to your former self." —*Ernest Hemingway*

Many mistakenly believe leadership is activated as soon as one receives a sense of *calling*. They think that an individual can start governing immediately. But this is rarely true.

World-changing leaders typically emerge after an extended period of development. Their grace usually comes to fruition over time.

- What are you doing to grow and advance in your areas of responsibility?

- Why is self-leadership critical to success? Why do you need to invest in your own insights and maturity?

Many called to lead don't understand that developing as a leader is a process. There are no overnight successes. Identity and character have to be developed. Strength typically comes with time. No one can rush it.

Doing

> I've missed more than 9000 shots in my career. I've lost almost 300 games. 26 times I've been trusted to take the game winning shot and missed. I've failed over and over and over again in my life. And that is why I succeed.
>
> –Michael Jordan

Leadership isn't just positional; it's also functional. It's more than what one *represents*; it's also what is *done*. People who transform the world are those who are not afraid to act.

Responsibility

> "A hero is someone who understands the responsibility that comes with his freedom." —Bob Dylan

Leadership isn't about seizing power or establishing the rules; it's about serving others. Individuals aren't placed into positions of authority to throw their weight around or boss underlings. They have arisen because of a willingness to carry the load. They are obligated to preserve and protect the community.

It comes down to this: If you aren't willing to pay the price and take responsibility for others, you're in no position to lead. If you aren't ready to manage difficulties, you aren't positioned to take the helm. Leadership is a *sense of responsibility* in the *hands of capable individuals*.

- What are your most irresponsible decisions? What assumptions led you to make those choices?

- What do you need to do now that you should have been doing all along?

- What can you do this week to own your share of responsibility instead of putting the burden on others?

Productive

'The way to get started is to quit talking and begin doing."—Walt Disney

In addition to the magnitude of responsibility, we have other factors to consider. When people talk about God's commands, they usually discuss several things. However, one responsibility is rarely acknowledged—productivity.

The initial command of Scripture to the man and the woman was tied to the importance of fruitfulness. The Lord declared, "Be fruitful and increase in number. Fill the earth" (Genesis 1:28 NIV).

The heavenly Father made it clear that he expects his sons and daughters to be productive. This command involved more than birthing children. As his "image-bearers" (Genesis 1:26), we're called to demonstrate all of who God is within the natural order.

- Do you have a mindset to work?

- What does it mean to be productive in your sphere? What are some ways that you can push the ball down the field?

- Are there any ways to increase productivity?

Diligent

> "If a man's gift is . . . leadership, let him govern diligently" (Romans 12:6, 8 NIV)

Leaders are eager to run beyond the finish line. It's not just *who you are* and *what you do*, but also *how you do it*. World-changers go as far and as fast as necessary.

If an individual has received a leadership gift, they should discharge every duty they have been entrusted with. There are no excuses for laxity or inaction. Those in charge should be ready to brandish their strength.

- What lessons are there to learn from Ulysses S. Grant as he fought against the Confederate armies? Although the general wasn't the most gifted planner or strategist, he was willing to press in for the win.

- What areas do I need be more diligent in?

Accessible

> "Real leadership is leaders recognizing that they serve the people that they lead." —Pete Hoekstra

Along with other duties, a leader should also be accessible. This can be awkward and inconvenient, but authorities who make themselves available transform institutions.

When a leader doesn't stay in touch with what's happening, they lose the pulse of the organization. They make decisions that don't consider what's happening on the ground.

Accessible leaders make a real difference. They are close to the heartbeat of the enterprise.

- Are you accessible to the right people?

- If not, what do you need to do?

- Are you managing your time well? If so, how are you doing this?

- Do you keep some of your time unscheduled? Are you allowing space for reflection and the assimilation of lessons learned from your experiences?

Accountable

"Leaders inspire accountability through their ability to

> accept responsibility before they place blame."—Courtney Lynch

Leaders *do* and *go*. They're innately *productive, responsible, diligent,* and *accessible*. But there's another component —*accountability*. No matter how fast or far a pioneer runs, they remain answerable to the mission and the organizational stakeholders. Power divorced from partnership, covenant relationship, and accountability will often result in disaster.

- Who are you accountable to?

- Do your attitudes and actions align with organizational values? Are you accomplishing the mission? What results are we producing?

- What outcomes have you made yourself accountable to? Reflect on a few of them below:

- Who are some of the stakeholders and leaders that you are accountable to?

Action is essential. Society isn't asking for any more theorists and talking heads. They're crying out for forerunners who accomplish what needs to be done. They want people who take action.

Even in the face of hardships and opposition, leaders find ways to faithfully execute. The passionate ones can't stand on the sidelines; they are ready to move ahead. They won't rest until they see everyone mobilized.

3

LEADERSHIP MECHANICS

> Leadership is lifting a person's vision to high sights, the raising of a person's performance to a higher standard, the building of a personality beyond its normal limitations. —Peter Drucker

Leaders must move beyond theories and move into the realm of practical application. Ideas have to work in the actual world.

Based on exchanges with entrepreneurs, educators, and influencers, I've noticed seven leadership mechanics. These action points aren't exhaustive, but they provide a useful place to start a discussion.

Leaders perceive, initiate, fund, disrupt, empower, protect, and inspire.

1. Perceive

> The greatest leaders mobilize others by coalescing people around a shared vision. —Ken Blanchard

Influencers without a wide-angle lens have a tough time getting their organization off the ground. Vision isn't rooted in a leader's personal preferences or selfish ambitions. It has little to do with the interior world of an individual. Instead, it draws on a deeper awareness that transcends every day affairs. Vision is rooted in the eternal destinies of nations, cities, and enterprises.

King Solomon declared: Where there is no vision, the people perish (Proverbs 29:18 KJV). Another translation renders it this way: "Where there is no revelation, people cast off restraint." Societies need leaders who can help them see the loftier purposes. Vision is the overriding concern.

Elsewhere in the Bible, God revealed the following to the prophet Habakkuk: "Write down the vision and clearly inscribe it on tablets, so that a herald may run with it" (Habakkuk 2:2 CSB).

The revelation needed to be clarified so the entire community could implement it. If they wrote it down, the vision would become a matter of public record and anyone could act on it.

Seeing is not just about seeing ahead. It's also about seeing behind. It is important to know where you've been so you find your way forward.

- Ask, "Who have we, as an organization or community, been when we've been at our best?"

- Consider value systems. What does your organization

stand for—and what does it stand against? What problem is it trying to solve?

- Who or what is your organization challenging? Why is it contending in this way?

- Now, what do you see before you?

- Do you live in the present?

- What are the present conditions and problems?

Confirmation bias is the inclination to gather, interpret, and recall information in a way that supports one's pre-existing beliefs. People tend to ignore contrary information and interpret ambiguous evidence as supporting existing beliefs.

- Have you allowed confirmation bias to affect your decisions? How is the way you as the leader think and process information affecting your organizational culture?

- What could the future look like?

- What do you want your future to look like?

- Vinyl record albums came back in vogue. Could anything else that is "expired" make a come-back?

Some ideas and expressions are inevitable. Eventually they are going to rise to the surface. The author Victor Hugo once said, "All the forces in the world are not so powerful as an idea whose time has come."

2. Initiate

> "A good plan violently executed now is better than a perfect plan executed next week."—General George S. Patton

Leaders are individuals that are ready to initiate things. They are not afraid to get things off the ground, even if the execution is imperfect.

- What could you launch today?

- Who could you borrow from or learn from to take your project forward?

- Are other opportunities available?

- Are you pushing your ideas further, making them more concrete. Are you going from hunches to notions to ideas to theories?

- Are you documenting your ideas, sharing your thought patterns and having your theories collide with the real world? Are you testing and proving what you believe to be true?

You probably already know this but leadership is hard work. Football great, Vince Lombardi said, "Leaders aren't born, they are made. And they are made just like anything else, through hard work."

3. Fund

> Empty pockets never held anyone back. Only empty heads and empty hearts can do that. --Norman Vincent Peale

Another important component of leadership is the reality of finances. People who change the world understand the importance of funding.

Some people perceive all the world's goods—wealth, land, honor, etc.—are limited in supply. A limited good mindset believes that the universe is one of fixed and limited supply. Within this mindset, life is zero-sum game—if I give it away, I cannot benefit. Everything must be horded.

But the abundance mindset believes that economies scale and that rising tides lift all boats. In this mindset, generosity is considered good and powerful. I believe that this is a better way of looking at the world.

- Do you have a lack mindset? Do you see the world from the perspective of limited goods?

Enterprises are typically funded by sales, subscriptions, fees, memberships, tickets, rentals, grants, venture capital, investments, patronages, or with churches and non-profits, free-will offerings. One or more of these is how a team funds their operation.

- So, how does your organization generate income?

- Is this approach a viable long-term financial model? Can you expect it to work in the months and years ahead?

- How do I currently obtain funding? Is this approach working?

It is important for every leader to continue to think about the realities of finances.

4. Disrupt

> "When something is important enough, you do it even if the odds are not in your favor." —Elon Musk

Leaders are willing to disrupt the pre-existing order and overturn the apple cart. Sometimes the systems and processes need to be changed.

Dr. Martin Luther King Jr. altered the way injustice was dealt with in America. This civil rights icon not only gave the marginalized a voice, but they also transformed the attitudes of a generation.

In the mid-twentieth century, oppressed Black Americans had only two options. They could react in violence, with grim repercussions, or lie down in the dirt and keep the peace. But this all-or-nothing approach left little recourse for Black Americans.

Dr. King pointed out a third way—non-violent protests. He took the Old Testament concern for justice and joined it with the New Testament message of love. King introduced a whole new social and political narrative that disarmed his oppressors. He knew that whoever captured the hearts of the people also had their ear.King said,

> There comes a time when people get tired of being trampled over by the iron feet of oppression. There comes a time, my friends, when people get tired of being plunged across the abyss of humiliation. . . And I want to say that we are not advocating violence. . . We believe in the teachings of Jesus. The only weapon that we have in our hands this evening is the weapon of protest. That's all. . .My friends, don't let anybody make us feel that we are to be compared in our actions with the Ku Klux Klan or with the White Citizens Council. There will be no crosses burned at any bus stops in Montgomery. There will be no white persons pulled out of their homes and taken out on some distant road and lynched for not cooperating. There will be nobody among us who will stand up and defy the Constitution of this nation. We only assemble here because of our desire to see right exist. My friends, I want it to be known that we're going to work with grim and bold determination to gain justice.[1]

King wisely reconstructed the narrative. He and his colleagues were not lawless; they were Christians taking the higher stand. No one can cogently condemn a peaceful advocate for the marginalized. Those who show restraint and self-discipline in their pleas will not be ignored.

- Martin Luther King Jr. disrupted the world. What are some other examples of innovation that you've witnessed?

- Are you exposing yourself to new inputs and new situations, and challenging yourself to find more interesting ideas?

- What needs to be disrupted today?

- What are the rules and assumptions your industry operates under? What if they are wrong?

- If all the leaders of your organization got fired and a new team was brought in, what would they do?

Leaders have to keep thinking about disruptions and what it means to innovate and grow. Advancement rarely comes without a serious shaking.

5. Empower

> "The greatest leader is not necessarily the one who does the greatest things. He is the one that gets the people to do the greatest things." —Ronald Reagan

One of the most significant tasks for an established leader is to champion those who are emerging. Bill Gates, the architect of Microsoft computers, said, "As we look ahead into the next century, leaders will be those who empower others." Sam Walton, the founder of Walmart, felt the same way. He said,

"Outstanding leaders go out of their way to boost the self–esteem of their personnel. If people believe in themselves, it's amazing what they can accomplish."

Leaders need to work with and empower others. Sadly, most organizational heads design things for people rather than with them. Building on the future is not merely sharing responsibility or involving younger leaders in operations. While there are advantages to this, the next generation needs a strategic investment.

- Do you work well with others? How effectively do you form partnerships? Do you know how to communicate and engage?

- As a leader, are you paying enough attention to your team?

- Who could you invest in this week that would really make a difference?

- Consider what things might look like for someone else. Answer this question, "What is it like to work with me?"

The famous CEO of General Electric, Jack Welch, had the following to say, "Before you are a leader, success is all about growing yourself. When you become a leader, success is all about growing others."

6. Protect

> "People sleep peaceably in their beds at night only because rough men stand ready to do violence on their behalf."—George Orwell

Organizations and communities will be attacked in this contentious age. The only way to avoid criticism is say nothing, do nothing, and become nothing.

Strategic leaders aren't willing to do this. They know that standing out can make you a target and they do it anyway. They stand strong and will guard their enterprises.

- Have you experienced any opposition?

- What are some of the kinds of things that you have been criticized or attacked over?

- What have you done to guard and protect what has been entrusted to you?

- How would you distinguish between weakness and wickedness?

Leaders fight for their families and their organizations. They stand strong in the face of opposition. This role can never be undervalued.

7. Inspire

> "Leadership is the art of getting someone else to do something you want done because he wants to do it."
> —General Dwight Eisenhower

Many of the leadership models over the years have been coercive. Control and force defined authority. But this is not always the best approach. Leaders need to find more inspiring ways to motivate people.

- How do you pivot from coercive leadership approach to a aspirational model?

The Apostle Paul writes, under the inspiration of the Holy Spirit: "Although in Christ I could be so bold and order you to do what you ought to do, yet I prefer to appeal to you on the basis of love" (Philemon 1:8-9).

- What does it mean to appeal to people on the basis of love?

- How did Martin Luther King Jr.'s approach to social justice disarm his enemies?

Leadership is about influence, not control. Those who are changing the world don't lead like the pagans.

Processing the Seven Mechanics

Every leader, no matter how gifted, will ultimately come up short. Even those with the most extraordinary abilities will not be able to accomplish everything alone—particularly with so many disruptions. Many challenges seem to lie before us.

Those at the helm need co-learners, co-laborers, and collaborators to assist with the work. Leaders benefit immensely when they draw from

- Mentors
- Models
- Partners
- Friends

Mentors

> "A mentor is someone who sees more talent and ability within you, than you see in yourself, and helps bring it out of you." — *Bob Proctor*

Mentors are mature leaders who impart high-level wisdom and guidance. These individuals are further along in the journey and can help navigate uncharted waters. Those who have been where a leader is traveling can provide valuable insight.

It's satisfying to sit down with a mentor, but their understanding can be passed on indirectly through audio recordings or books. Emerging leaders need someone to teach them along the way.

- What does a mentor look like? What qualities do you look for?

- List some of the people who have been mentors in your life?

- Who would you like to have as a mentor?

Models

"Imagine for yourself a character, a model personality,

whose example you determine to follow, in private as well as in public."—Epictetus

Models flesh out needed outcomes. These people put theory into action. They embody the values. We all seek an example, and they provide this for us. We learn more easily from observation than from articulation. A great example is twice as valuable as well- intentioned advice.

A leader can find plenty of suitable models in books, but they're best found in local relationships. Locate a transparent person whose life can be thoroughly examined. Never underestimate the relevance of demonstrated examples.

- What are some of their qualities that you would look for in a model?

- List some of the individuals who have been models for you?

- Think of someone else who might have these qualities.

Partners

> "Great things . . . are never done by one person. They're done by a team of people." —Steve Jobs

Partners hold up a leader's arms as Aaron and Hur did for Moses. (See Exodus 17:12.) The Old Testament lawgiver could not have carried out God's mission if it weren't for the contributions of these men. They kept Moses strong.

Partners work alongside a leader and do some following: resource, manage, and carry out urgent duties. They are irreplaceable supporters who uphold the mission of the institution.

- What does a partner look like? What are some of their qualities?

- List some people who have been partners in your life?

- Is there anyone that you should talk to about partnership?

Friends

> "The friend in my adversity I shall always cherish most. I can better trust those who helped to relieve the gloom of my dark hours than those who are so ready to enjoy with me the sunshine of my prosperity." — Ulysses S. Grant

Friends have the most to offer a besieged leader. They provide a kind word and loving support. These peers create a safe environment to talk. Friends are less focused on the organization than on the individual leading it. For them, it's not business, it's personal.

Jesus revealed in Scripture, "No one shows greater love than when he lays down his life for his friends" (John 15:13 ISV). Giving of yourself for others is the essence of friendship. Everyone needs a faithful confidant who stands with them through life's difficulties and trials.

- What do friends look like? What are some of their qualities?

- List some of the people who have been friends in your life?

- Are there friends that you're ignoring? Write down the names of people who stand with you.

Never undervalue the contributions of others. Each of us receives extraordinary benefit from *mentors, models, partners,* and *friends*. These allies bring gifts to the table that we desperately need.

Divine Favor

> What I am now I am by the grace of God. The grace he gave me has not proved a barren gift. I have worked harder than any of the others—and yet it was not I but this same grace of God within me. (1 Corinthians 15:10-11 Phillips)

As vital as it is to get help from others, the ultimate leadership catalyst comes from somewhere else—divine favor. When grappling with responsibilities, we must lean into the inexplicable wonder of grace.

Contemporary leaders benefit from the wisdom, gifts, and competencies of others, but they will get nowhere without the Lord's favor. One will invariably make mistakes and come up short. A godly leader does all that he or she can but depends on God to make up what's lacking.

- Are there any areas where you have witnessed the favor of God in your life?

- Take a moment and pray for God to help you in the areas of need.

Great colleagues and fruitful execution are vital parts of leadership, but so is casting everything on Jesus. He's more than enough to carry you through. In him, you can endure hardship and discharge all the duties you have been entrusted to accomplish.

---

1. Dr. Martin Luther King, Jr., "Montgomery Improvement Association Mass Meeting," Holt Street Baptist Church, Montgomery, Alabama (December 5, 1955). https://kinginstitute.stanford.edu/king-papers/documents/mia-mass-meeting-holt-street-baptist-church#fn1

4

CONCLUSION

Sometimes the world changes so drastically that the ground moves out from under you. In these periods, the finest education, tools, and strategies no longer help.

The citizens of Choluteca, Honduras, encountered this two decades ago. In the late 1990s, the Hazama Ando Corporation constructed a steel bridge that could withstand gale force winds in this Latin American nation.

Not long after the bridge's completion, a Category 5 hurricane hit. As torrents of rain fell, Honduras was swamped. Although this edifice withstood the storms, its resilience hardly mattered. The Choluteca River had been re-routed in the deluge.

- What bridges do you need to leave behind?

- Are you prepared to move beyond everything you know?

God is at work. Though we might not see it, he's restoring beauty and wonder. In this age, he is releasing grace like never before. Many men and women are rising above the fray and discovering their destinies. Leaning into this moment, leaders are asking questions, making connections, and seizing opportunities.

A glorious future is unfolding. Mercy and grace are on display.

Gifted sons and daughters are commissioned to reflect God, accomplish exploits, and revolutionize the world.

God is asking each of us to take a second look at what he's doing.

In a topsy-turvy world, he's unleashing creators, educators, ministers, and entrepreneurs. All of us are a vital part of heaven's advance. How thrilling to be on the cusp of this earth-shattering shift.

- What did you learn about yourself by reading this book?

- What is your biggest takeaway?

- Are there any areas that you would like to work on in the weeks and months ahead?

We're moving forward in a disruptive era. We must continue pivoting and re-imagining a world of beauty and goodness. It's time to lean into the shift.

About J.D. King

J.D. King is an author, speaker, publisher, and leadership ooach. In addition to consulting, developing training resources, and writing books, King has composed blog posts garnishing over 1.5 million page views.

King equips leaders through the *Revival Network* and is an associate pastor at World Revival Church in Kansas City, Missouri.

To find out more about J.D. and how he could speak to your group, visit him online:

Email: jdking@wrckc.com
Blog: jdking.net
Bookstore: TheResurgenceStore.com
Twitter: @jdkinginsights
Facebook: authorjdking

Made in the USA
Monee, IL
03 March 2022

92136005R00049